FACING THE PROBLEMS OF HUMANITY

CARL KENT

Facing the Problems of Humanity

Copyright © 2022 by Carl Kent.

Ebook ISBN: 978-1-63812-533-4
Paperback: ISBN: 978-1-63812-499-3

All rights reserved. No part in this book may be produced and transmitted in any form or by any means, electronic, or mechanical, including photocopying, recording, or by any information storage and retrieval system, without permission in writing from the copyright owner.

The views expressed in this work are solely those of the author and do not necessarily reflect the views of the publisher hereby disclaims any responsibility for them.
Published by Pen Culture Solutions 11/23/2022

Pen Culture Solutions
1-888-727-7204 (USA)
1-800-950-458 (Australia)
support@penculturesolutions.com

CONTENTS

Facing the Problem   i

Acknowledgments   iii

Chapter 1:
The Basic Problem   1

Chapter 2:
Drugs   13

Chapter 3:
Sex, Divorce, and Abortion   23

Chapter 4:
Racism   29

Chapter 5:
Noninvolvement   35

FACING THE PROBLEM

WE FACE PROBLEMS TODAY IN every area of our lives. Christians know that "Jesus is the answer" to all our problems. By this, they mean that if the gospel was preached to all men and all men came to the saving knowledge of Christ, there would be no more problems.

All men will not respond to the Gospel. Experience shows that few accept the truth than reject it. Christians will always be a small group in society. The majority, in other words, will never be "converted" until Jesus returns. If all men became believers, we would still have problems because, as believers, we are not perfect. Look at your own church; look at yourself.

Does this mean that we are to give up the struggle? We think not. We believe God wants his people always to be an influence for good. We do not believe he wants us to give up teaching Sunday school, witnessing, doing visitations, singing in the choir, or actively serving him in other areas of the ministry.

This is how "Christ is the answer." He is the answer as we apply to the problems of our time. The principles he advocated and used, the principles embodied in God's Word, the Bible. The more these principles are applied to conditions today, even believers, the better off society will be.

ACKNOWLEDGEMENTS

WE APPRECIATE MATERIALS FROM CHRISTIANITY today and time and life, materials from the *World Book Encyclopedia*, and materials from the Christian.

CHAPTER 1

The Basic Problem

CHRISTIANS TODAY AGREE THAT GOD is in heaven but find it hard to believe that things are all right with the world. It is more honest to admit how much is wrong with our generation's world.

Every age is inclined to believe it is turning on the brink destruction. "The world is going to the dogs" has been a constant theme among older observers of the status quo. Even great men of today said, "The times are out of joint." Our grands prayed and sought God about the wickedness of the future generation, the high cost of living, and the great extravagance in government.

In no other generation, however, have the problems been either as numerous or as intensified as they are today. One sees signs everywhere of a world culture involved with so many serious problems that many "experts, scientists, economists, sociologists, and medical men confess they see no way out. The world's clock will soon strike midnight and bring civilization, as we know it, to an end. We are thinking in terms of the next twenty years." After that, well, we're just not counting on anything after that.

What's wrong with the world? Here is a partial list of problems men face today:

- *Communism is a form of government. Once, long ago, a communistic community was one in which all the people owned everything together. No one had private property except perhaps his clothes and a few personal possessions.*
- *The world's population is increasing as supplies of food dwindle, confronting millions with starvation within a few decades.*
- *Poverty increases with population growth. Even in the United States, there are poverty pockets in both suburban and rural areas.*
- *Drugs are on the increase and getting a stronghold on American teens. They affect the mind that will determine what the next generation is like. Youth are turning to alcohol, which already kills 30,000 persons a year on United States highways and accounts for hundreds of millions of dollars a year in losses.*
- *Crimes have increased. Even in areas, people are afraid to leave their homes at night because they might be held up or mugged by youths who need money to pay for drugs to which they are addicted.*
- *Terrorism is on the increase, "senseless" bombings by "activists," and increasing of threats. More in the first three of 1970 than in all of 1969.*
- *The gap between the generations widens. The present generations are convinced that adults have failed and that the new generation must bring about achange.*
- *There was talk of a lower hemline on women, but we have heard no upset that interest in promiscuous sex is declining. Pornography in magazines, books, and materials are at an all- time high.*
- *Blacks have made great strides in their struggle for equality in the United States, but much remains to be done in eliminating racism.*

— *Inflation has become reality. Labor is asking for all-time high wages, and stockholders demand a good profit.*
— *Through carelessness, greed, and ignorance, men are degrading God's world in such a way that we are actually in danger of running out of water to drink and air to breathe.*
— *Taxes have reached an all-time high that some economist tells us we have passed the point of no return and that national economic ruin is unavoidable unless drastic actionis taken.*
— *As church merges and gobble up on one denomination after another, the people of the United States are staying away from Sunday school and church in even larger numbers. More and more people indicate that the church is having a positive influence on the world about it.*

WHAT CHRISTIANS HAVE TO SAY

You will agree that the problems we have and a number of others that could readily be added are important and that they deserve the attention they are beginning to get from many people. Many Christians believe that most of these issues are basically moral problems. We know that this is a correct observation. If we know that the Bible contains God's moral law and revelation of hispurposes both for mankind and for the world, we can expect it to say something about the dilemma that confronts us.

What then should the church do? If the church does not help Christians to think openly in the light of God's Word about these problems, where are believers to look for such direction? AreChristians merely to wash their hands and await the millennium?

We believe that God has a message of hope for today's disordered world and that the future he offers is the only valid hope for mankind. We believe that it is possible to isolate a single underlying cause of the problem with which men are grappling and to point also to the basic remedy. We shall examine some of the problems in a Christian perspective—the only perspective valid for who believes that the God of the Bible is the sovereign Lord of the universe. This is the only perspective that offers support for an optimistic view of the "situation."

What is behind it all? If we were to conduct a poll and ask people to name one man's basic problems, we would get various answers. If you were to ask, what accounts for all the crises in thisgeneration, people would say the following:

— *Ignorance*
— *Prejudice*
— *Mistakes*
— *Selfishness*
— *Impatience*
— *Carelessness*

These answers would be true to a degree. All these elements, and many others, lead to the problems confronting our world. The term that comes closest is selfishness. If men were unselfish, most of our problems would vanish. Selfishness is involved in almost every one of the many difficulties we face.

Sin is the breaking of the commandment that God has given us. Sin is coming short of thestandards God has set. Sin is selfishness, putting one's self in the place of God.

We know from our experience that we are frank with ourselves and that we are sinners bynature. We know from the Bible that we are likewise sinners by nature.

"I was shapen in iniquity, and in sin did my mother conceive me," confessed by King David.

Sin is the cause of all men's problems, troubles, and mistakes. But sin is an unpopular word to say. It has not been dropped from the dictionary, but it has disappeared from the vocabulary of many theologians and preachers. It hurts a man's ego when someone calls him a sinner, and many considerate folks don't want to hurt anyone's ego. So they don't call people sinners, but instead, they use the terms we have suggested. A person is ignorant or mistaken or selfish or careless, but he is not a sinner.

Other religions say that every person is a child of God. What he needs, according to their view, is not the new birth, for he is already in God's family. He needs education. If we convince him that he is God's child, then he will act as a child of God should act. Education, not salvation, is the answer.

They say the facts don't support their theory. Men need something more than knowledge of what they ought to do. They need a new nature. The life of God in them that will make them want to act as they know they should. They have the know-how but not the want to.

WHAT SIN DOES TOMEN

Man's problems are symptoms of his sinful state. Sin changes the contact between man and God. It breaks the human-divine relationship so that man is out of contact with God, not aware of God's revelation, indifferent to God's purposes, and not at unity with God's will.

He has lost touch with the holiness of God that would motivate him or, with the power of God, would enable him to live in line with God's standards. When a man's life is not rightly related to God, it is not rightly related to other men either. Correct a man's relationship with God, and you will have some basis for following that he will be rightly related to his fellowmen. If all men were rightly related to one another, the world's problems would vanish.

Meantime, man's sinful nature shows itself in the selfishness he is concerned with. He put himself in front of all others, even ahead of God, in order to gratify his own needs. He becomes materialistic, pleasure seeking, self-centered, sensual, unfair, and given to anything (crime, terrorism, drugs) that may give him new self-satisfaction for which he wants.

REMEDY FOR SIN

Imagine a town with a water supply that has been polluted. This problem could be resolved in the obvious ways. Each family would attach every faucet with a filter that would strain out impurities. The other would involve installing one big filter at the source of the supply or eliminating the source at the well.

Men today are struggling with many aspects of one basic problem. They are dealing with racism, violence, noninvolvement, drugs, and many other symptoms. They are putting filters on a hundred faucets instead of getting at the pollution. The root cause, the basic cause is man's sinfulness. Man's way to solve society's problem is to attack each individual problem by itself while carrying on a program of mass education that hopefully will result in a new order.

Man's emphasis on education has resulted in what we call the "knowledge explosion." Men know twice as much today as they knew ten years ago. Lack of knowledge is not our crucial problem today. What men lack is understanding to use their knowledge in such a way that they do not destroy themselves with it. No school offers a course in wisdom. Man's only source for wisdom is God. God gives it to those who are rightly related to him. God's remedy for sin is Christianity—the salvation of a person.

The source of salvation is the Lord Jesus Christ, who came to this world as God in the flesh not only to reveal God to man but to set a perfect example of holy living, but to die as the sacrifice of man's sin and make salvation available to as many will accept it.

Since sin is man's basic problem and God's remedy for sin is salvation, we need to ask ourselves, "What is a Christian?" A person who has accepted salvation. The term is used loosely today and often improperly.

Here are some statements usually true of Christians, but not every person. To whom one or all these statements apply is necessary a Christian in which the term is used in the New Testament:

— *He is a member of a local church*
— *He claims to be a believer*
— *He is "religious," he reads the Bible, attends church, and prays.*
— *He believes that certain teachings are true. Being a Christian is as follows:*
— *A personal relationship to God as his child*
— *Possession of a new kind of life—here and now as well as eternity.*
— *Being indwelt by the Holy Spirit. The spirit of Jesus Christ, his power, his wisdom, and his love.*

Being a Christian then is having the right relationship with God. Jesus helps the Christians to face life with peace, joy, confidence, poise, and power.

A Christian can bring the wisdom of God to bear on his own problems and on the problems of the world around him. Being a Christian does not ensure one having any problems. God does not promise that his children are going to escape illness, accidents, losses, or disappointments. He does assure them that he will help them live in victory, in peace of mind, and joy of the heart. Even indifficult circumstances, God puts before a Christian the highest standards of morality and spirituality. The standards are revealed in God's Word, the Bible.

God does require obedience to a set of commandments as the price of salvation, for salvation is a gift, and we cannot earn it. God gives to Christians authority over the pull of their unspiritual natures and a desire to live the life that will please him. He enables us to be a better person, have better marriage partners, better employees, and be a better employee, better neighbors, better church members, better residents, and better citizens of the nations.

He transposes us from the realm of the problem to the realm of the problem solver. He converts us from the negative to the positive. We no longer contribute to the world's problems or sit on the sideline and wait for our Lord's return, but we are able to make a dynamic, positive contribution. Being a Christian in a day like ours is a wonderful thing. We are suggesting that Christian sought to use ordinary means at their disposal to meet the needs and problems of people around them. They must not stop with ordinary means, for the Christian answer goes deep into the root cause of our problem, while the ordinary means often deal with symptoms.

This is a definite promise if men will put God in first place; he, in turn, will provide them with the necessities of life. The church may use ordinary means at her disposal as giving food or night lodging.

1. *Even when all members of a group are believers, there are often problems. Some local churches may have no function or controversy, but they are few and far between. The failure comes because Christians do not always live by the*

> *truth they believe. When this happens, their relationship to God, as well as to man, gets "out of kilter." If you have any doubts about this, read 1 Corinthians and think about the problems that beset the Christian church in Corinth—carnality, division, incest, false teaching, and the like. If all Christians were perfect, the New Testament epistles, all of which addressed to believers, need hardly have been written. These letters are warning for God's people, who are not yet perfect. Becoming a Christian is the step toward right living, but we deceive ourselves if we think that a believer will do everything right.*
> 2. *Christ is the answer to all man's problems, but this answer will not be complete until Jesus's return and sets up his kingdom on earth. Then, and only then, will we have peace on earth, along with perfect justice, worldwide righteousness, brotherhood, and holiness. Our effort will never usher in the glorious time when the kingdom of this world shall become the kingdom of our God.*

God's people are to preach the gospel to every nation, offering salvation to all who will accept it by putting their trust in Jesus Christ. They are to teach men not only to believe but to do all thingsChrist has commanded (Matthew 6:10). There is room (in the church) not only for the evangelism of the lost but also for every philanthropy and usefulness. There may be the most aggressive work for the masses. The ministry of healing for the sick and suffering and the most complete provision for charitable relief.

BECOMING A CHRISTIAN

There are steps that lead into the Christian life. A person may take them at any time and in anyplace. Here's how:

1. *Know the gospel. Christianity is based on certain events. The birth of Jesus Christ, the Son of God, his death on the cross for the sins of the world, and his resurrection from the grave. The fact that these things really happened is what makes Christianity unique among the world religions.*
2. *Believe the gospel. You must not only know the truth about Jesus Christ, but you must accept it as true. God cannot and will not help you if you think the gospel is a lie (Hebrews 11:6).*
3. *Depend on the gospel. You must not only know the truth and believe the truth, but you must trust yourself to the truth. You do this by telling God, and you must be sincere, of course, that you realize that nothing in you is worthy of his approval and that if you are to be acceptable to him, it will be through Jesus Christ's death. If you are honest in committing yourself to Jesus Christ, trusting God to forgive you because his son died for our sin, you will become "anew creation" (2 Corinthians 5:17). Christ will come to live in you.*

This generation is one of the most complex issues confronting our nation today. Some of the areas in which our young people are involved are drugs, crime, sex, and others. The generational gap, is there one? If so, what is it? There are people who think that the generational gap is new. It's always been here. They feel even though its manifestation change from one decade to the next. Others are not sure. They point to problems peculiar to our time: drugs, spiraling juvenile crime, changing sexual standards, and growing involvement of youth in social issues.

The church, meantime, struggles to help teenagers find themselves to point security in Christ and to reconcile them with their parents. What is crucial for Christians to understand why young people feel and behave as they do and approach the situation with Christlike love and patience, prayingthat the Holy Spirit will bring healing and meaning to young and old alike.

WHO IS INVOLVED?

It is hard to assess how many young people are involved in various manifestations of rebellion against their elders. No one family or area can be considered typical.

1. *Thanks to television, tape recorders, record players, mass circulation magazines, and newspapers, no teenagers are untouched by pervasive youth characters of our day because of modern communications, style can be instantly mechanized. Protest movements are well publicized and quickly.*
2. *Though there are still pockets of poverty, food, clothing, cars, and entertainment has been accessible to many young people. Well-off parents have provided the means for their children to have almost anything they want. One of the facts has emerged from student violence is that organizers, in many cases, do not come from the ghetto but from wealthy families.*
3. *Most young people today are well-educated. They have been exposed, at an early age, to the failure of our adult society to solve some of the basic problems. They soon learn that manyadults have bad ideas, that they give way to financial and political pressures, and that appeal to the youth to behave is, in many cases, a mockery consequently. Many youth soon becomecynical and take the dropout route.*

But this is not true of all young people. To keep the picture in balance, we need to remember that a majority of those who will reach age thirty in this decade will probably never have smoked marijuana or engaged in a public demonstration and will generally adhere to the moral values of their elders.

Drugs are big with young people, even down to high school level. Drug usage is more than a habit. It is an extremely complicated social problem. Why young people go for drugs is hard to say, exactly would include disaffection with the world as a whole, wanting release from every day tensions.

Studies show that drugs users are often from middle and upper-middle class families. They are students of social science living in or near a large urban center.

No young person is really safe from drugs. There is a great social pressure at least to try smoking marijuana. It's not hard to find Christian young people who indulge.

CHAPTER 2

Drugs

THE WORST SICKNESS IN AMERICAN history is the current drug crisis. Number one crime problem is illegal dope, for which the United States is the number one customer. A news magazinecalls marijuana our other enemy.

With alarming speed and force, the problem has spilled out of ghetto and skid row into the mainstream American life. Drugs have gone up into society and down into the grades, out into the suburbs, and deeper into the cities, especially the inner cities.

The total direct and indirect cost of drug abuse in money, lives, health, productivity, social breakdown, law enforcement, family relation, and mental, moral, and spiritual damage is already staggering, and it is still spiraling.

Auto accidents attributable to drugs are increasing. Theft and prostitution generated to support drug habits are beyond calculation, but in New York City, such thieves and heroin addicts alone are thought to amount to two million a year. More than one thousand young people there have died from this drug in 1969. A terrible aspect of the problem is that youth are the primary victims.

WHY USE DRUGS

Many circumstances, pressures, and influences lead to drug use. This reason given includes the search for pleasure, expression of rebellion, using out of curiosity, and search for intellectual and/or spiritual reality. Among claims made for drugs are that they expand the mind, intensify senses, induce inner peace, create harmony, promote love and emotional sensitivity, give meaning and insight, full from "hang-ups," help release the "real me," reveal truth, reality, and beauty, offer salvation, an escape from the "unreal" world of hypocrisy and conformity, and stimulate sexual desires.

Regardless of how foolish these claims may be, we should approach the drug problem, and especially drug users, with humility and honesty, remembering Paul's warning to the Christians at Rome, "Lest we find that we who judge practice the same things" (Romans 2:1 NAS).

Our culture over many decades has become progressively drug-oriented. The varieties and quantities of legalized drugs and prescriptions are increasing phenomenally. Americans included are taking more and more drugs for more and more problems. Our society is already a drug culture, for which adults, not youth, have set the pace. Most of us are involved in the drug problem morethan we may want to admit. Tobacco contains both poisonous and habit-forming drugs. Fortunately, much popular and government attention is being focused on tobacco.

Alcohol, still our number one drug problem, not only exceeds tobacco's physical harm but attaches to the mind as well. Intake of alcohol has been chronic in the United States for years, but because most Christians are well-informed on this issue, we shall not consider it here. Caffeine is a drug found in coffee, tea, chocolate, and cola. It is by far the most common and widely used stimulant in the world. It is mild but habit-forming, which accounts to a large extent for the popularity of the food and drinks that contain it. Caffeine is not in the same category as alcohol, hard drugs, or even tobacco, but it is does cause physical and emotional harm—nervousness, irritability, etc. Christians who use caffeine should do with humility.

THE REAL DANGER

What are the causes that control our desire for artificial ease, pleasure, and performance? They are, for the most part, the same causes that are behind hard drug use. Medical and reasonable personal use expected drugs are only one of man's latest idols, viewing himself as basically an animal with no value or purpose, except those he may create or discover for himself. Similar to man, distorted ideas about God and himself are his ideas about truth. Having rejected God's Word, man is left on his worn resources.

He has no way of knowing where to look for truth or knowing when he has found it. As far as aperson can tell, one source of truth is as good as another, so he naturally relies on the one that promises what he wants to hear. Most dominant philosophy of modern man is self-willed, standardless, and most indefinitely variable. Most pop and psychological art, as well as hard rock music, are basically extensions of this philosophy. Like hallucinogenic drugs but through different means, they shatter and benumb nerves and break patterns and relationships. In short, they make a frontal attack on order, reasons, meaning, and understanding. It is no coincidence that standardless living and drug use are both rising at the same time. Nor is it coincidental that the generation so largely permitted if not taught to have its own way. Yet a person who ignores God's way not only has a poor idea of what he needs but can't even be sure of what he wants because they do not believe there is any purpose or meaning to life; they see no way to "ruin"it.

These are specific causes:

1. *Accidental addiction has long been a problem. Medical use of narcotics to relieve pain on the battlefield, in surgery, for cancer patients, etc. sometimes leads todependence.*
2. *Careless and indiscriminate prescription of powerful drugs. In fairness to doctors, it should be noted this is usually at the insistences of thepatient.*
3. *The illegal sale of legally manufactured drugs is of major importance. Authorities estimate that fully half of the barbiturates, amphetamines, and tranquilizers manufactured by licensed pharmaceutical companies find their way into the legalmarket.*
4. *Social acceptability has contributed to the increase of drug use. Even narcotics, especially the hallucinogens, are taken at parties where "getting high" or "tripping out" is accepted. "Pot" parties are rapidly becoming standard for the fast and sophisticated high school, college, and jetsets.*
5. *Many adults set a poor example by their own indiscriminate reliance on drugs, prescription, or otherwise. The major difference between parent and child is it that for the parent, drugs are more often a private crutch while for youth, they are usually a social crutch. Parents and general adult apathy are high on the list of causes. Indifference often hides a false and harmful sort of "trust."*

Closely related to indifference is parental pride reflected so often in the notion expressed or implied that "my child wouldn't do anything like that." Christians, above all, should realize thattheir not can sin but are in line toward it (1 John 1:8). Parents were invited to learn in confidence whether their children were involved. Only twenty bothered to check.

EFFECTS OF DRUGS

Some drugs do not always cause immediate harmful side effects or "bad trips." On occasion, pleasant and relatively harmless experiences are effective "bait" to users, just as an occasional win is bait to a gambler.

More serious than the physical harm of drugs is the psychological. Like alcohol, drugs most often affect the mind before the body and the higher parts of the mind before the lower. They quickly take a person out of the driver's seat of his own life.

Some areas in which drugs affect the body are as follows:

— *Judgment—impaired judgment is one of the first effects of most drugs. And the more impaired his judgment, the less chance of the user has of even being aware he has a problem.*
— *Creativity—a psychiatrist asked thirty-six artists of varying styles to try their talents under LSD. Virtually all of them experienced, by their own judgment, a marked decline in skill.*
— *Reality—a drug user forfeits his ability to see, smell, taste, hear, feel, and understand or explain anything "like it is." There is no way to determine, of course, but it seems highly probable that a user is upset of his own "trip" is unintentionally distorted.*
— *Will power—even when conscious of reality and of right and wrong, a user rapidly loses ability to make choices*

and may often find himself doing things which, even at the moment, he does not want to do.

— *Individuality—far from helping a person discover "who he is," drugs tend to abolish both self-awareness and individuality. The user never knows which is the "real me."*

— *Maturity—as a means of escape, drugs are a "coward's approach to life," a substitute for real living. They stifle ability both to face and to cope with life. An assessment who is already immature is thereby more susceptible to drug use. And one who is "on" drugs tends to become further self-centered, withdrawn, and aimless.*

— *Psychosis—it is not rare for heavy drug users to experience identifiable psychosis such as paranoia, guilt, complex, identity loss, or psychotic panic—induced, aggravated, precipitated or imitated by the drug. Drugs can cause "instant insanity."*

The significant thing is that all dangerous drugs—from barbiturates to heroin—tend to cause desire for continued use. Of major concern is drug escalation. All drugs begin to lose their "kick" after continued use. The only "solution" is to advance to stronger drugs. The milder drugs break one's resistance to the harder ones.

As terrible and dehumanizing are the physical and psychological effects of drugs, moral and spiritual damage is worse. The intoxicating euphoric, distorting, and debilitating effects of drugs on the brain are as close as anything physical can come to touching directly man's spirit. Whenever man dehumanizes by himself or others, God, in whose image man is made and whose son died on man's behalf, is outraged. It is through his will that a man may "believe unto salvation." Obey God and follow the Lord.

Anything that attacks or distorts a person's will is therefore utterly evil. Narcotic, hallucinogenic, and psychedelic drugs are diabolical barriers between men and God.

- *General values—a strongly addicted person values a fix above anything else. Eating, sleeping, working, friendship, reputation, and appearance all pale inimbalance.*
- *Morals—with loss of willpower comes loss of our personal and social "guard rails." Because drug use soon becomes extremely expensive, most boys are forced to stealing and girls eitherto stealing or prostitution or both to support the habit.*
- *Peace—in light of reality, it seems that the rock and the clenched fist are more appropriate symbols of the drug culture than is the flower.*
- *Love—the idea that drugs enhance any kind of love is perhaps the supreme myth of the drug culture. Though it is persistently and sincerely believed by many users.*
- *Life—drugs cause rapid decrease in general life interest and respect for oneself as well as for others. Both suicide and homicide rates have raised drastically in every drug are anti-life.*
- *God—drugs have been used in cult worship for thousands of years. Satan's influence in drug use should be evident to a Christian. Christians who work closely with drug users impact that biblical doctrine, and morals are usually among the first standards rejected.*

WHAT CAN A CHRISTIAN DO?

- *First, believe that something can be done. The idea that nothing can be done is unbiblical, unspiritual, and irresponsible.*
- *But, on the other hand, avoid false optimism. There is no panacea for the drug problem since it is related to many other problems, a number of which have already been mentioned. The latter must be fought on many fronts.*

— *Realize that the problem is not basic or practical but moral and spiritual. Above all, present Christ as the one who gives victory and new life with purpose and with the power of the Holy Spirit to overcome the root cause, which is sin.*
— *Recognize the hand of Satan in the drug problem and rely on the Holy Spirit's direction, especially in dealing with drug users. Here are some areas in which a Christian can show his concern and effort:*
— *Education—it is important to teach the dangers of drugs. But we must go beyond merely giving facts and include teaching of values and moral standards.*
— *Law—we should push for laws which are adequately enforced and are effective means of helping control drug use.*
— *Spiritual solutions—Christians must make every effort to hold and defend biblical faith, especially the foundational, absolute truths. Relativism is the friend, and propositional truth is the enemy of drug use.*
— *Love—is of supreme importance. Love that includes not only affection but genuine interest, knowledge, and understanding. You can't achieve these without spending time with your children.*
— *Discipline—should be included under love, for the loving parent disciplines his child (Hebrews 12:6). "Train up a child in the way he should go, and when he is old, he will not depart from it" (Proverbs 22:6). Parents need to abide by and claim this promise.*
— *Example—discipline of children is of little value without the self-discipline of parents. Children are much more inclined to follow their parents' example than be guided by mere verbal principles.*
— *Trust and Confidence—parents should trust their children in areas where the young persons are informed and experienced. This does not include blindness to a young person's ability to do something wrong.*

- *Explanation—parents should give reasons for what they teach and expect of their children*
- *—explain, not simply lament, the drug problem.*
- *Responsibility—teaching children and young people to take responsibility and to do things which are necessary but unpleasant is good prevention against the spirit of escapism upon which much drug use feeds.*
- *Challenge—the "idle mind" has always been a problem and needs to be met with challenging worthwhile activity. On the other hand, however, there is the growing problem of pressures: academic, social, parental, and athletic. Challenge upon many young people to overachieve. Unchallenged leads to boredom and desires for excitement, and over challenged leads to anxiety and frustration. Both extremes provide fertile grounds for drug experimentation.*
- *Prayer—only God can meet the full needs of our children, and only God can be with them continuously. Committing them daily to his care is not only the most spiritual but also the most practical thing any parent can do for their children.*

CHAPTER 3

Sex, Divorce, and Abortion

WHAT GUIDELINES ARE THERE FOR some scriptural thinking about marriage, which is one of the sociological foundations of our culture? What does the Bible say about love, marriage, and divorce? Does God's word deal with abortion?

GET A PERSPECTIVE

In the beginning, God created life, love, sex, marriage, and reproduction (Genesis 1:37; 2:18–25; 28). He sustains a relationship to God and is answerable to him. He is the object of God's affection and of God's communication.

1. *Natural revelation—this includes anthropology, biology, psychology, and sociology—any effort on man's part to discover the whys and wherefores of the world around us, which is evidence of its creators (Romans 1:19;20).*

2. *Specific revelation—the Word of God and the living word, who became a man (John 1:14), to reveal God to us (v.18). The scriptures, inspired and illuminated by the Holy Spirit and Christ himself (Hebrews 1:2), show us far more of God's nature and personality, of course, than we could ever glean from nature.*

We shall consider both God's natural revelation and his writings as they bear on our subject— life. One common idea of life is embodied in the expression we so frequently hear: "It's my life. I can do what I want with it and live any way I choose." There is just enough truth in this statement to make it misleading. We are constantly making choices, and these have direct and indirect individual and collective consequences. It should be equally obvious that:

— *There are sharp limitations to life*
— *My life is subject to many circumstances over which I have little or no control but which may have profound effects*
— *Though I may follow the path of my choosing, and once I select a certain path, I cannot evade the consequences of what choice I make.*

A Christian believes that life is both a gift and a loan from God. In a way, God gives us our lives to direct and enjoy, but in another sense, we are stewards of our lives which belongs to him. We are not our own, but we bought are with a price (1 Corinthians 6:19; 20). Life is a loan for which we must give an account. It is a privilege, but it is also a responsibility.

LOVE

It isn't easy to define love, for it has a variety of characteristics. One thinks of mutual attraction, mutual affection, and mutual response to the needs and wishes of the other or deep concern for and a commitment to the welfare of the other. One thinks of Jacob's love for Rachel, so great that his seven years of servitude for her seemed to him like a few days (Genesis 29:18; 20).

SEX

God created human life in the form of two sexes. Since God could conceivably have created human beings to reproduce by dividing in the middle like the amoeba, we may ask, "Why did he make thetwo sexes as we know them?" The Bible reveals two primary purposes for sex:

1. *Companionship (Genesis2:18)*
2. *Reproduction (Genesis1:28)*

They ranked in this order because this is the chronological order in which they occur and also because this is the apparent order of their importance. Companionship is the purpose in view in God's statement, "It is not good that the man should be alone. I will make him a help meet for him (Genesis 2:18)." This statement, of course, was made before the creation of Eve. The statement about reproduction, "Be fruitful and multiply" (1:28) was obviously made to Adam and Eve ("them") after Eve had been brought into being.

If a married couple consider their companionship the basic element of married life and continue it through the marriage, when the children have left them, the couple still have unity of their relationship which will grow closer and more meaningful each.

If, on the other hand, a couple value reproduction above companionship, their children tend tobecome all-important. The couple builds their lives around the children rather than around one another. After the children leave, the couple may face tragic loneliness and an intolerable vacuum.

For one thing, they share their similarities. One of these is mentioned in the New Testament, which says husband and wife are "heirs together of the grace of life" (1 Peter 3:7). This indicates both partners in a marriage share a conception of life as God's gift. The sharing of similarities is seldom a problem. To share differences is more difficult, and it is here that marriage relationships may be severely threatened and broken or, on the contrary, enriched and deepened. The sexes are appropriately fitted for one another's needs.

DIVORCE

Divorce is an extremely controversial issue in Christian circles today. Generally speaking, there are two extreme views on divorce, with a variety of in-between positions all held by apparently sincere believers.

The first view is that divorce is allowable only on grounds of adultery. Many add to this condition the stipulation that neither party is to be allowed to marry and that the individuals involved to hold any official position in the church. Second view is that though the scripture teaches marriage as lasting, ideally, and forever, a married person is entitled to break the union by divorce if his partner persists in actions or attitudes of distortion, persistent isolation, or extreme physical or mental cruelty, that completely block the marriage relationship.

It should be suggested, therefore, that in teaching and motivating people, we should hold ideals goals before them and not compromise. However, in dealing with specific, tragic, and complicated instances, we must remember that human beings are finite, and we must be compassionate.

REPRODUCTION

The second main purpose of sex is reproduction. Here, again, is a combination of responsibility and privilege in scriptural command to replenish the earth.

This command was given when the earth was relatively empty and overpopulation was not a problem. Today with population bringing the threat of gradual human extinction by starvation and/or pollution, Christians must be especially sure of God's will with regard to reproduction. Psychologists have pointed out a number of rather questionable motives, sometimes unconscious for the conception of children, including the following:

— *Ignorance and carelessness and perhaps misguided belief that God will prevent a pregnancy in spite of carelessness*
— *A parent'sc onscious or unconscious need to fulfill a frustrated ambitiont hrough the child*
— *Effort to stabilize a shaky marriage and to forestall separation or divorce by keeping the other partner tied*
— *Loss of a marital partner's affection, leading to transfer of affection to children*

These conditions lead people, at times, to think of abortion.

ABORTION

Abortion is a far more controversial issue in Christian circles today than it has ever been before. This fact is, at least in part, due to these "cut and dried" understandings that have prevailed in Christian circles.

— *If abortion occurred spontaneously, especially in the fact of all reasonable efforts to prevent it, it was apparently God's will.*
— *If abortion was strongly recommended by one or more qualified professionals in order to save the life of the mother, it was probably God's will.*
— *A part from the above, abortion was equivalent to taking of human life, and this is under no circumstances justifiable. A Christian is in danger of being caught up in the movement which demands abortion on request, which could readily degenerate into abortion upon whim and fancy.*

We can all know that God is still guiding us today. Let us keep our hearts and minds open to both the absolute revealed truth and also to the relative issues of this changing world in which he has seen fit to place us (John 17:15).

CHAPTER 4

Racism

RACISM HAS PRODUCED UNCONTROLLABLE PASSIONS in our time. The slightest remark giving evidence of disrespect can cost men their jobs, can ignite a riot, and can bring the operations of a university to a halt. Emotions run high around the term "racist" and "racism."

All this makes calm stud of the subject difficult. Most of us have our minds firmly made up and view new facts as threats. And many of today's problems regarding race spring partially from ignorance.

Evangelical Christians particular need to bring their dedication, compassion, and faith to this national crisis. We need to hear again our Lord's words: "Blessed are the peacemakers, for they shall be called the children of God" (Matthew 5:9). We need to acknowledge our role in this issue, either as part of the problem or part of the solution. We need to see our discipleship to Jesus Christtested in the arena of today'ssociety.

Riots in our cities, fair housing laws in our legislatures, and busing in our school systems have shown clearly that we are one society and that there is no place to hide from its problems.

WHAT IS RACISM?

Racism itself is an attitude which holds that a person is superior or inferior because of his race. Since this attitude is not founded in facts, it is a form of prejudic which dislikes a person for no real reason. As some would put it, racism is "being down on something you're not up on." It is usually leads to efforts to control or suppress the race considered inferior. Racial prejudice involves both attitudes and beliefs. We can attack false beliefs by information and education, but attitudes are much harder to uproot.

The gospel of Jesus Christ is powerful, however, and it offers men a totally new life and a newperspective. The Holy Spirit wants to change a believer so completely that we can only compare the change to a "new birth" (cp. John 3:7). The gospel, in short, offers a man a new heart and a new mind. His nature ideally is transformed by the power of God. New attitudes should ultimately and inevitably result.

A PREVALENT IDEA

The idea that one race is superior to another is especially ugly in our country because it discloses the conflict between our American ideal of "liberty and justice for all" and our American practice of "liberty and justice" for all. What we claim and what we do obviously clash. Racism expresses itself in three ways. One is in words. This includes criticism, jokes, and threats. Another is through unfair customs and laws aimed at certain races. Segregation by law in housing, recreation, and transportation are familiar forms of discrimination. Still, another expression of racism is physical violence, such as bombings or lynching. Any one or all of these expressions of racism may be directed toward a group or toward an individual because he is a member of that group.

An evangelical Christian may be a party to racism by unkind jokes, by comments designed todegrade or hurt another, or by approval of discrimination in housing or on jobs. A Christian can actively help overcome racism through integrated worship, tutoring programs in the inner city, voting for equal opportunities, and the like.

RACISM EVERYWHERE

Through prejudice is no doubt as old as man, racism as we know it today arose in the sixteenth century with overseas conquest by European countries. Slave ship crewmen were among the firstwhite men to develop racist attributes. As hard as their own were, they knew they were better off as black men and women herded like cattle below deck, and so they felt superior.

With the growing impatience of cotton in the late seventies, the South turned increasingly to slave labor. More cotton meant that additional slaves were needed. Slavery came to an end in the United States only after the costly Civil War, which turned brother against brother and spilled blood across our country. Lincoln's Emancipation Proclamation ended slavery as in institution, but racist attributes lived on segregation, and discrimination replaced direct physical bondage.

The black struggle against discrimination broke out with new vigor in the fifties. The Supreme Court's ruling on May 17, 1954, struck down legal support for segregation of school facilities.

REASON FOR RACISM

The reason for racial hatred, we learn from scripture, lies in the sinful self-centeredness of the human soul, "All have turned aside together they have become useless... Their feet are swift to shed blood, destruction, and mainly are in their paths" (Romans 3:12; 15; 16 NAS). All this means is that where racist views are part of the tradition of a country, mere membership in a church, even in an orthodox one, will not free a man of these prejudices, only the convicting power of the Holy Spirit can do that.

When a person becomes a Christian, he is not immediately made perfect in attitude or in anything else, rather he is justified or counted perfect (Romans 4:3; 24). He is born into spiritual life not made mature or complete, like a newborn baby, he must develop. The greater part of the New Testament is devoted to teaching Christians how to grow up spiritually (cf. Ephesians 4:13). Christian growth is largely the process under the Holy Spirit's direction and power of putting off the attitudes and habits of old life (4:22) and putting on those of the new (4:24). A Christian indwelt by the spirit has the potential of a truly righteous, God like life.

CHURCH AND RACISM

Most churches long ago so lowered their standards of membership and dropped the practice of church discipline so completely that they have no basis for excluding a staunch racist from membership.

Many American churches reflecting the world about them have surrendered biblical doctrine after biblical doctrine until many truths have been forgotten. In such churches, the teachings of the Bible against discrimination (e.g., Acts 10, Romans 2:10, James 2:1) and on the oneness of believers in Christ (Galatians 3:28) are overlooked or rationalized.

American churches have often appealed to supposed "biblical evidence" to prove that blacks are inferior. One argument insists that blacks are descendants of Ham and therefore destined by god to be servants forever. This myth is based on Genesis 9:20; 25. Where Noah, awakening from a drunken stupor, pronounced or cursed upon Canaan, the son of Ham, saying "Cursed be Canaan, a servant of servants shall be unto his brethren."

The Bible contains a wealth of teachings that bear on the race question. The foundation of these teachings is a biblical view of God, who is righteous, just, and merciful. He expects his children to be the same. He told the people of Israel, "You shall be holy, for I the Lord your God am holy" (Lev.19:2). One of god's purposes for his people is that they become partakers of his nature (2 Peter 1). In other words, become like him. This has great significance for race relations, for since God loved the world (John 3:16), he expects us to love all men too.

The Bible makes clear that God is our father. If we are his children by faith in Jesus Christ, oursavior. John wrote, "As many as received him (Jesus), to them gave the power to become the sons of god, even to them that believe on his name" (John 1:12). Justification by faith and forgiveness of sin, so central in the gospel, are meaningful only if we recognize that God accepts men purely on the basis of grace, apart from human qualifications. If we refuse fellowship to men for whom Christ died, we are excluding men whom God has included.

CHAPTER 5

Noninvolvement

SOMETIMES WE ARE TEMPTED TO think of our faith as a way of escape from the harsh demands of life. God has always been a fortress for his people in time of trouble and danger (Psalm 18:2). He most certainly is still our refuge (Psalm 46:1). The Holy Spirit is our comforter (John 14:16; 18), as well as our guide, our teacher, and the one who imparts spiritual life.

There is much more to life of faith than seeking shelter and security. David, who often spoke of God as his refuge, was not a man to run away from problems. He found God's help most real and meaningful when he faced the foe. Whether the enemy was Goliath, Saul, the Philistines, or evil tendencies of his own heart (cf. Psalm 51). The "peace" the disciple experienced in the Garden of Gethsemane while Jesus was organizing in prayer was not God's peace. Today, many believers know little about getting into the arena instead of retreating for a weekend or a week of strengthening themselves spiritually and to plan together the retreat with only their own problems. To stagnate, they fail when it comes to opposing evil and injustice.

OUTWARD CAUSES

There have always been obstacles to helping; for example, there are legal reasons for some or no involvement. Liability laws often work against the "good Samaritan" who may be sued and heldaccountable for harm or complications using from his well-intended help. Some people are suspicious of help. They either think the person is trying to take advantage of them or is helping from a purely selfish motive.

Others resent help because of pride and self-sufficiency. Accepting help, to them, indicates weakness, irresponsibility, or dependence. Still, others are sensitive about people "butting into" their business. The see any help as unwarranted influence in their personal affairs.

A final obstacle is the attitude of some onlookers. Perhaps because of ignorance of the circumstances or perhaps because of feeling guilty for not doing anything themselves to help. They call us "do-gooders, busy bodies," or worse. Even when we really want to help then, it is not always easy.

INNER CAUSES

Wanting to help and taking the initiative, however, are still the hardest parts of being a goodneighbor. Even our attitudes toward these reasons can keep us from doing what we should. Lack of application by neighbors, for instance, is sometimes a detriment, but it should not be an excuse.

No one who is indifferent to the needs of others can claim the support of either God's word orGod's spirit for his attitude.

Instead, he stands under their judgment. Right doctrine and right standards are no substitute for right love and right service.

God's commands to believers to serve him, and others are almost beyond counting. Many of these biblical commands are "standing orders" that is applicable under all circumstances. Jesus "went about doing good" (Acts 10:38), so did the apostles. John tells us that a Christian who says he loves God but does not love his brother is a liar. Loving our Christian brother and our fellowmen and expressing our love in action are what Christian involvement is all about.

INVOLVEMENT PARABLE

The parable of the Good Samaritan answers two questions: "Who is my neighbor?" and "How should I be a neighbor?" Jesus answer to the first was that our neighbor is anyone who needs our help whether we live next door to him or pass him on the street accidentally—whether his skin isblack, white, or another hue.

God's people are not to fold their hands, relax, and do nothing until the rapture. They are to occupy until he comes (Luke 19:13). God gives his servants different callings (Romans 12:3–8; 1 Corinthians 12:28–31). He does not call all of us to serve in the same ways, but he calls all of us toserve, not in ways that please us but in his way.

God makes persons different in character and personality. Some Christians are natural extroverts. They find it easy to mingle with others, to make friends, and to be leaders. Other persons are more introverted. They work best alone or with a few close associates. In spite of differences, however, God has given some calls to all believers. He calls all of us to lose our lives for Christ

(Matthew 10:39), to love our neighbor as ourselves (Luke 10:27). The commands in God's word for his children to be "involved" are countless and clear.

PLANNED INVOLVEMENT

One mark of a Christian is that he goes about doing well, after the example of his Lord (Acts 10:38). There are many ways in which we can plan to be involved. There are constant or recurring needs in any neighborhood, church, or community. Some of the needs are obvious. Others must be sought out.

Usually, our planned involvement isn't of such long-range consequences, but it needs to start in exactly the same way as theirs did—where we are, with what we have, and with the need that is closest to us.

Naturally, we cannot be involved with every need around us. In fact, there is so much to be done that we should pray, "Show me a need to serve in your name," but rather, "Father, show me which need you want me to help meet our talents or training may help us decide how and where weshould become involved for theLord."

On the other hand, we sometimes discover talents simply by willingness to take on a job that needs doing. In working with people, it is often our attitude more than our talents that meet their real need. Just being with a person and talking with him may be the "cup of water" he needs.

UNEXPECTED INVOLVEMENT

First, we must be open and sensitive to others and able to recognize their needs. We must build a reservoir of love, knowledge, and insights which God may use as the needs arise.

No human ministry or no period of service in God's work has ever approached in importanceJesus's earthly ministry. Nor has any other ministry been so limited by time, only three and a half years to call and train his disciples and to preach and to heal. Yet the gospels are filled with accounts of how the son of God willingly, patiently, and ungrudgingly took time immediately, toheal the widow, forgive a prostitute, or talk with a Roman, a Samaritan, a child. Even the agony of the cross, Christ met the needs of the thief and of his mother. Did race or nationality make anydifference to him? How important are our schedules compared with his?

In the light of the Bible's teaching and especially in light of Jesus's examples, it is clear that the unexpected needs that confront us are not interruptions of our work for the Lord. They may interrupt our plans, not suit our convenience, and radically conflict with our ideas about spiritualpriorities. They may even interfere impartially with other important work for God.

God approves guide for what we should do for someone else, assuming of course, that it is in harmony with other biblical teaching. If we have even been in great pain or faced in financial crisis or lost a close loved one or been ostracized or maligned, then our experience can offer excellent suggestions for our helping to others in such circumstances. In cases where our own experience is lacking, a concerned and consecrated imagination is helpful. Just trying to put ourselves in another's shoes is a starting place for understanding and a step toward being helpful.It is a spiritual starting place (Matthew 7:12),too.

One of the serious frustrations of "law and order" today is unwillingness of "decent citizens" to testify whether to convict the guilty or exonerate the innocent. Failure to witness is, in reality, false witness because it supports falsehood by silence. Biblical warnings against false witness from the Ten Commandments through the prophets, gospels, and epistles are abundant and familiar. Willingness to testify in court is not only a Christian's civic duty but his moral duty as well.

When we look at society and the things that are happening around us, family problems and drugs are on the increase, but there is hope when we allow God to be incontrol of our lives.

I believe this book will help the ones that are struggling with habits that they can't keep orcontrol; by reading it will help them understand who God is and that he loves them.

I want society to know that there is hope with the problems that we are facing and that we need each other because we cannot make it in this world by ourselves. We need strength and help from God.

www.ingramcontent.com/pod-product-compliance
Lightning Source LLC
LaVergne TN
LVHW051217070526
838200LV00063B/4946